Welcome to my kitchen!

The kitchen is my most favorite and treasured place to be in my home.

My earliest childhood memories are of me and my maternal grandmother cooking in her kitchen together. She could turn the simplest, freshest ingredients into mouthwatering food that would warm your heart and your belly.

This is my story of love for her and a celebration of the woman who shaped my cooking journey.

Table of
CONTENTS

03

SAVORY SIDES

Backyard BBQ Beans 40
Grilled Breaded Eggplant 41
Zucchini Fritters 42
Stovetop Grilled Zucchini w/Shaved Pecorino Romano 43
Artichoke Casserole 44
Roasted Asparagus w/Balsamic Drizzle 45
Easy Peasy Peas w/Onions 46
Stuffed Artichokes 47
Bacon Infused String Bean Sauté 48

04

POTATO SIDEKICKS

Sweet Potato Medley 50
Golden Roasted Crispy Potatoes 51

05

VIBRANT FRESH SALADS

06

SWEET TEMPTATIONS

Introduction

It all started in her kitchen...

Cooking with my grandmother left a mark on my heart that will always feel like home. She was my favorite person on this earth. The time we spent together was so very precious. Being with her in her kitchen made me feel safe, loved and so very special. Her kitchen was a sanctuary for me that signified an unwavering love for her family.

When I am cooking in my own kitchen, I often think of her and remember her using only the freshest ingredients to create the most delicious meals. To this day I grow a gigantic vegetable garden every summer because of her.

The belief that food is not just merely sustenance but a language of affection is how I live my life.

/2

There's nothing like homegrown produce

I remember our trips to the grocery store together. We would head back to the butcher counter and she would buy only the freshest cuts of meat to cook with. While she didn't have a lot of money, food quality was a priority to her. I am of the same belief for my own family.
When my grandmother died in 2000, she took all of her recipes (and my heart) with her. As I sit here today, I am eternally grateful for the time I had with her and for the gift of her cooking. Writing this cookbook has brought me so much joy, as I have reminisced with each line I have written.

There were so many times my mom and I would try to get my grandmother to write down her recipes, she would tell us to just watch her as she cooked. We would watch and attempt to write, but we just couldn't ever seem to do it. She measured with her heart, not with measuring cups.

My mom and I always ended up just watching her, soaking up her voice as she cooked and then we'd eat. We never wrote a single recipe down.

If you have a grandmother like mine, you know there's not much that can be duplicated and it always tasted better when it was made with her hands.

Watching her cook gave me such a sense of respect for the kitchen, and taught me at a very young age, that food truly is love.

As I grew up watching my grandmother and my mom cook, I knew I would do the same for my own family.

I will never forget my mom always having dinner made, and we ate as family every single night. My mom cooked with love exactly like her mom (my grandmother) did.

From the time I was 11 my mom started having me prep dinner with her.

It felt like such a honor to be able to do that with my mom. I loved being a part of feeding our family. It's one of the things that shaped me into the wife and mom I am today.

.

When I married my husband 30 years ago, I knew with all of my heart that I would be the wife and mom that cooked every day. From very early in our marriage, I shopped almost daily, (I still do) for fresh ingredients for our meals. I very rarely, if possible, ever use anything frozen or from a can.

I have always laughed because I tell people, "Jesus wants me to be in the kitchen cooking all day" , because anytime I try and take a shortcut, it ends up biting me where the sun doesn't shine.

When I had my kids, my world became "Food is Love" .
I wanted them to have the exact same home cooking experience I had growing up. Home grown veggies from our garden and the freshest of meals at our dinner table, every single night.

From the time my kids were tiny little guys, I had them in the kitchen with me while I cooked.
It was a bonding time for us, and a way for me to introduce them to my happy place. My oldest son is an amazing cook, and a food lover to his core. Both of my boys appreciate the value of food and
the importance of family meal time.

Until the day my kids moved out we sat down for dinner together
as a family, every single night. It was non-negotiable in our home,
and something I am so proud of as a mom. It's one of the things I
miss most as an empty nester. But you better believe I bribe them to
come home with my cooking, every chance I get!
There is nothing I love more than when my kids come home to eat, and
ask me to make their favorites.

My husband always joked with me as our kids grew up
that "I ruined our kids with food" . It makes me giggle to this day,
because what he's referring to, is the fact that our kids wouldn't
dream of eating off a kids menu in a restaurant when they were little.

/7

Our kids were the ones asking for the salmon or the chicken vesuvio off the menu, not the chicken nuggets.

I wrote this cookbook for my kids. My love language has always been food, and being able to write this cookbook has made that love language grow even deeper.

This cookbook is a culmination of my recipes, my grandmother's, my mom's and my mother- in-law's. All the women I love, are and were the most amazing cooks and their love language has always been food as well.

My philosophy of cooking, is that nothing has to be perfect. If I'm baking...yes, that's different. But cooking doesn't always have to be perfectly pretty to be full of flavor. Sometimes things don't look like the pictures, and that's okay! The flavors are there, and most importantly, the love is too.

Being in my kitchen brings me immense joy and solace. I do my best thinking and I also like to pray while I cook. Talking to God helps quiet my mind, as I create in my kitchen.

This cookbook is a tribute to the lessons my grandmother taught me in her kitchen- patience, generosity and the joy of feeding others. It is an homage to the woman whose legacy continues to inspire me every day.

I hope you find value in my story and in my recipes. I hope you feel a new sense of warmth as you cook. The love of food is what it's all about. Simple, fresh ingredients, that can create a love language like no other.

Xo,
Shelly

SHELLY'S *Kitchen* ESSENTIALS

~ PLEASE for the love of all things holy...
use fresh garlic.
Do not use garlic from a jar or a tube..
Once in a while I will use
granulated garlic. It can
add great flavor when I want a light garlic flavor.
~PLEASE use fresh basil. Dried basil doesn't
even have the same flavor.
It's just an unnecessary dry spice
lurking in the spice rack.
~Plain breadcrumbs are best.
Add flavor with your spices.
~Use freshly grated parmesan cheese.
(I actually only use pecorino romano,
but that's just
a preference of taste, and I can't eat dairy)
~Choose fresh over frozen when possible.
~Get yourself a food mill or an immersion blender.
~Bake from scratch...Skip buying store
bought sweets.
~Use good extra virgin olive oil. I use the
brand called Violi. Nothing ruins a salad or a dish
more than bitter olive oil.

A FEW LAST THOUGHTS BEFORE
WE COOK TOGETHER ⋯

• WHEN I SAY "A FEW TURNS"
OF OLIVE OIL, I LITERALLY MEAN
TAKE THAT BOTTLE THAT HOPEFULLY
HAS A NICE WIDE SPOUT, AND POUR
IT AROUND IN A CIRCLE INTO YOUR BOWL
OR INTO YOUR PAN.
•OLIVE OIL IS REALLY MEASURED WITH YOUR HEART,
NOT A MEASURING CUP.

•YOU'LL SEE I DO NOT USE A LOT OF SALT.
YOU DO YOU, BUT I DON'T SEE THE NEED.
I WOULD RATHER USE SALT JUST TO TASTE.

•PLEASE, PLEASE, PLEASE STOP
USING OREGANO IN YOUR PASTA SAUCE.
PASTA SAUCE IS NOT PIZZA SAUCE.
I SAID WHAT I SAID. PERIOD, NO EXCEPTIONS.

NOW LET'S GO COOK!

1

DINNER
Delights

THE HEART OF THE KITCHEN
BEATS WITH LOVE

SIMPLE ROASTED PORK TENDERLOIN

INGREDIENTS

2 PORK TENDERLOINS (ABOUT 1 LB EACH)

1 TEASPOON PAPRIKA

1 TEASPOON GRANULATED GARLIC

1 TEASPOON GRANULATED ONION

1/2 TEASPOON DRIED THYME

1 TEASPOON SEA SALT

1/2 TEASPOON PEPPER

1 TEASPOON DRIED OREGANO

2 TABLESPOONS LEMON JUICE

2 TABLESPOONS OLIVE OIL

COOKING PROCESS

• PREHEAT OVEN TO 400 DEGREES

• COMBINE DRY INGREDIENTS & SET ASIDE

• PIERCE TENDERLOINS ON ALL SIDES AND RUB THE OLIVE OIL INTO THE MEAT.

• SQUEEZE THE LEMON JUICE ONTO THE MEAT AND THEN PAT THE DRY SPICES ON ALL SIDES.

• PLACE THE TENDERLOINS ON A BAKING SHEET AND BAKE FOR 25-30 MINUTES UNTIL THE INTERNAL

TEMP IS 160 DEGREES.

• ALLOW THE MEAT TO REST FOR 10 MINUTES AND SERVE

CHICKEN CUTLETS

There is nothing better than golden brown, crispy chicken cutlets. They are delicious alone, but can be used alongside pasta, or as chicken parmesan.

INGREDIENTS

- 4 THINLY SLICED CHICKEN CUTLETS
- 2 CUPS PLAIN BREADCRUMBS
- 1 CUP GRATED PARMESAN CHEESE
- OLIVE OIL
- 3 EGGS BEATEN
- 2 TEASPOONS GRANULATED GARLIC
- 1 TEASPOON SALT
- 1/2 TEASPOON PEPPER
- 3 TEASPOONS FRESH CHOPPED PARSLEY

COOKING PROCESS

- PREHEAT OVEN TO 350 DEGREES
- PLACE LARGE SAUTÉ PAN ON STOVE TOP AND POUR OLIVE OIL TO COVER BOTTOM OF THE PAN.
- COMBINE BREADCRUMBS, PARMESAN CHEESE AND SPICES IN A SHALLOW BOWL; SET ASIDE.
- BEAT THE EGGS IN ANOTHER SHALLOW BOWL.
- HEAT THE PAN TO MEDIUM HEAT.
- DIP EACH CUTLET INTO EGG AND THEN INTO BREADCRUMB MIXTURE. COAT COMPLETELY AND PLACE IN PAN.
- COOK UNTIL CRISPY AND BROWN ON BOTH SIDES AND THEN TRANSFER TO A COOKING SHEET AND BAKE FOR 20 MINUTES.

HEARTY CHICKEN STEW

INGREDIENTS

- 3 TABLESPOONS OLIVE OIL
- 2 TABLESPOONS TOMATO PASTE
- 1 ONION, CHOPPED
- 3 CLOVES GARLIC; MINCED
- 1 1/2 LBS BONELESS CHICKEN BREASTS
- 2 CARROTS; PEELED AND CHOPPED
- 2 CELERY STALKS; CHOPPED
- 1 TEASPOON DRIED THYME
- 2 BAY LEAVES
- SALT AND PEPPER TO TASTE
- 2 32 OZ CARTONS CHICKEN BROTH
- 1 CUP YELLOW POTATOES; PEELED AND DICED
- 1 CAN DARK RED KIDNEY BEANS; DRAINED & RINSED
- 1 CAN CANNELINI BEANS; DRAINED & RINSED
- 1/4 CUP FRESH PARSLEY; CHOPPED

COOKING PROCESS

- SEASON CHICKEN BREASTS WITH SALT & PEPPER.
- POUR 2 TABLESPOONS OF OLIVE OIL IN A PAN AND BROWN THE CHICKEN ON BOTH SIDES. REMOVE CHICKEN AND CHOP INTO BITE SIZE PIECES; SET ASIDE.
- IN A LARGE POT ADD ALL THE VEGETABLES, AND THE TOMATO PASTE. ADD IN ABOUT 1 TABLESPOON OF OLIVE OIL.
- COOK VEGGIES FOR 5 MINUTES.
- ADD PARSLEY, THYME AND BAY LEAVES.
- ADD CHOPPED CHICKEN IN AND POUR IN THE BROTH.
- BRING TO A BOIL AND THEN LOWER HEAT TO A SIMMER FOR 1 HOUR.
- SERVE WITH A SPRINKLE OF PARMESAN CHEESE.

INGREDIENTS

- 2 4-6 OZ PIECES SALMON
- 2 GARLIC CLOVES;CRUSHED
- 1 TABLESPOON BUTTER
- 1/4 CUP HONEY
- 1/4 CUP SOY SAUCE
- 2 TABLESPOONS LEMON JUICE
- 1 TEASPOON CORNSTARCH

SIMPLE SALMON

COOKING PROCESS

- PREHEAT OVEN TO 350 DEGREES.
- PAT EACH PIECE OF SALMON DRY.
- IN A SMALL SAUCEPAN MELT THE BUTTER, THEN ADD IN HONEY, SOY SAUCE, LEMON JUICE & GARLIC. ADD IN CORNSTARCH AND STIR AS THE SAUCE THICKENS.
- PLACE SALMON ON FOIL LINED BAKING SHEET.
- BRUSH SALMON WITH HALF OF THE SAUCE. SAVE THE REST FOR DIPPING.
- BAKE FOR 15-20 MINUTES.

INGREDIENTS

- 4LB WHOLE CHICKEN
- OLIVE OIL
- 2 STICKS BUTTER
- 1 TEASPOON SALT
- 1 TEASPOON PEPPER
- 1 TEASPOON GRANULATED GARLIC
- 1 TEASPOON OREGANO
- 1 TEASPOON PAPRIKA
- 1 TEASPOON PARSLEY
- 1/2 CUP CHICKEN STOCK

COOKING PROCESS

- PREHEAT OVEN TO 350 DEGREES.
- REMOVE ANY GIBLETS FROM CHICKEN AND DISCARD.
- MIX DRY INGREDIENTS AND SET ASIDE.
- RINSE AND PAT DRY CHICKEN AND PLACE ON A RACK IN A ROASTING PAN.
- RUB THE CHICKEN ON ALL SIDES WITH OLIVE OIL AND PAT DRY INGREDIENTS ONTO ALL SIDES.
- CUT THE BUTTER INTO CHUNKS AND SCATTER AROUND THE BOTTOM OF THE ROASTING PAN AND THEN POUR THE CHICKEN STOCK ON THE BOTTOM AS WELL.
- ROAST IN THE OVEN FOR 2 1/2-3 HOURS; INTERNAL TEMPERATURE NEEDS TO BE 165 DEGREES.
- REMOVE AND LET THE BIRD REST FOR 10 MINUTES.
- SLICE AND SERVE.

WHOLE ROASTED CHICKEN

There's nothing more wonderful than a home that smells of comfort food. A chicken roasting in the oven reminds me of a cold, snowy day when my boys were small. I took them to our local Polar Express train ride event on a cold, snowy, December day. After we got home, I roasted a chicken and the aroma as it cooked, made the house feel so warm and cozy.

DOMINIC'S CRISPY RICE PORK CUTLETS

> THESE PORK CUTLETS ARE MY OLDEST
> SON'S FAVORITE. IF I ASK HIM WHAT HE WANTS ME TO MAKE,
> THIS IS HIS ANSWER EVERY TIME.
> HE LIKES THEM NICE AND GOLDEN, ALMOST BURNT!

INGREDIENTS

- 2 LBS BONELESS THIN SLICED PORK CUTLETS
- FLOUR FOR DREDGING
- 3 TABLESPOONS LEMON JUICE
- 5 CUPS RICE KRISPIE CEREAL; GROUND INTO A POWDER WITH A FOOD PROCESSOR
- 4 EGGS
- 1 TEASPOON SALT
- 1/2 TEASPOON PEPPER
- 3 STICKS MARGARINE

COOKING PROCESS

- POUND EACH CUTLET BETWEEN PLASTIC WRAP.
- BEAT THE EGGS IN SHALLOW BOWL, ADD LEMON JUICE.
  PUT FLOUR INTO A SHALLOW BOWL.
- PUT GROUND RICE KRISPIES INTO A SHALLOW BOWL.
- DREDGE EACH CUTLET IN FLOUR, DIP IN EGG & THEN DIP AND COAT COMPLETELY INTO CEREAL.
- I DO ALL THE DIPPING AND SET CUTLETS ASIDE.
- HEAT A SAUTÉ PAN ON MEDIUM HEAT AND ADD THE MARGARINE ABOUT 2 TABLESPOONS AT A TIME. THIS IS WHERE IT GETS A LITTLE TEDIOUS...
- ADD THE CUTLETS TO THE PAN. DON'T CROWD THEM, DO JUST A FEW AT A TIME. KEEP ADDING PATS OF THE MARGARINE AS YOU COOK THE CUTLETS. YOU DON'T WANT THE BREADING TO STICK. COOK THEM UNTIL CRISPY, GOLDEN BROWN. 4-5 MINUTES PER SIDE.
- LAY THE CUTLETS ON A PAPER TOWEL LINED DISH AS THEY COME OFF THE STOVE.

INGREDIENTS

- 4 LARGE CHICKEN BREASTS
- 4 SLICES OF FRESH MOZZARELLA CHEESE
- 4 SLICES PROSCIUTTO
- 1 CUP PLAIN BREADCRUMBS
- 1 CUP GRATED PECORINO ROMANO CHEESE
- BALSAMIC GLAZE
- OLIVE OIL (FOR PAN, AND PASTE)
- SALT, PEPPER, PAPRIKA
- 1 PACKAGE FRESH SPINACH
- 2 GARLIC CLOVES; CRUSHED
- KITCHEN TWINE

STUFFED CHICKEN BREASTS WITH BALSAMIC GLAZE

COOKING PROCESS

- PREHEAT OVEN TO 350 DEGREES.
- POUR 1 TABLESPOON OLIVE OIL INTO A SAUTÉ PAN.
- CRUSH THE GARLIC AND ADD TO PAN ALONG WITH SPINACH.
- COOK UNTIL SPINACH IS WILTED. ABOUT 4 MINUTES; SET ASIDE.
- SLICE EACH CHICKEN BREAST LENGTHWISE FORMING A POCKET BIG ENOUGH TO STUFF.
- LAY ONE PIECE OF PROSCIUTTO IN EACH BREAST.
- MIX THE BREADCRUMBS AND OLIVE OIL INTO A PASTE AND SPREAD ON EACH BREAST.
- PLACE ONE SLICE OF MOZZARELLA, AND THEN A COUPLE OF SPOONFULS OF SPINACH INTO BREASTS.
- SEASON BOTH SIDES WITH SALT, PEPPER & PAPRIKA.
- TIE EACH BREAST WITH KITCHEN TWINE.
- HEAT OLIVE OIL IN A PAN ON MEDIUM HEAT AND ADD THE CHICKEN BREASTS. COOK UNTIL BROWNED ON BOTH SIDES.
- REMOVE FROM HEAT AND PLACE CHICKEN BREASTS ON A BAKING SHEET LINED WITH ALUMINUM FOIL AND BAKE FOR 30 MINUTES OR INTERNAL TEMPERATURE IS 165 DEGREES.
- REMOVE FROM OVEN AND DRIZZLE WITH BALSAMIC GLAZE AND SERVE.

COCONUT CRUSTED CHICKEN TENDERS

INGREDIENTS

- 1 1/2 LBS CHICKEN TENDERS
- 1/2 CUP CORNSTARCH
- 3/4 TEASPOON SALT
- 1/2 TEASPOON PEPPER
- 1 TEASPOON PAPRIKA
- 3 LARGE EGGS
- 1 1/2 CUPS SWEETENED COCONUT
- 1/2 CUP PLAIN PANKO
- VEGETABLE OIL FOR FRYING

COOKING PROCESS

- MIX CORNSTARCH, SALT, PEPPER & PAPRIKA; SET ASIDE IN A SMALL BOWL.
- BEAT EGGS IN MEDIUM BOWL.
- COMBINE PANKO AND COCONUT IN A MEDIUM BOWL AND MIX WELL.
- DREDGE CHICKEN IN CORNSTARCH MIXTURE AND SHAKE OFF EXCESS.
- DIP IN EGG AND THEN PRESS CHICKEN INTO INTO THE PANKO MIXTURE ON BOTH SIDES UNTIL COMPLETELY COATED.
- HEAT OIL IN A HEAVY SKILLET (MAKE SURE OIL IS 3/4 " DEEP OR MORE).
- ADD CHICKEN TO HOT SKILLET IN SMALL BATCHES
- COOK FOR 6-7 MINUTES ON EACH SIDE OR UNTIL COOKED THROUGH. [INTERNAL TEMPERATURE SHOULD BE 165 DEGREES].

HONEY MUSTARD DIPPING SAUCE

- 1/3 CUP DIJON MUSTARD
- 1/4 CUP HONEY
- 1/4 CUP MAYONNAISE
- 1 TABLESPOON WHITE VINEGAR
- OPTIONAL DASH OF CAYENNE

MINESTRONE SOUP

INGREDIENTS

- 3 STALKS CELERY; DICED
- 1 MEDIUM ONION; DICED
- 3 CARROTS; PEELED AND DICED
- 2 SMALL YELLOW POTATOES; PEELED AND DICED
- 1/4 HEAD CABBAGE; CHOPPED
- 1 CAN CANNELLINII BEANS; DRAINED AND RINSED
- 1 CAN DARK RED KIDNEY BEANS; DRAINED AND RINSED
- 1 SMALL ZUCCHINI; CHOPPED INTO BITE-SIZE PIECES
- 3 32 OZ CARTONS ORGANIC VEGETABLE BROTH
- 1 TEASPOON SALT
- 1 TEASPOON PEPPER
- 2 TABLESPOONS TOMATO PASTE
- 3 TABLESPOONS OLIVE OIL
- OPTIONAL TINY PASTA NOODLES OF CHOICE

COOKING PROCESS

- POUR OLIVE OIL INTO THE BOTTOM OF A LARGE STOCK POT.
- TAKE THE TOMATO PASTE AND MELT WITH THE OLIVE OIL. COOK FOR 1 MINUTE ON LOW HEAT.
- ADD ALL OF THE VEGETABLES AND THE BEANS AND SAUTE FOR 10 MINUTES ON MEDIUM HEAT.
- POUR IN THE VEGETABLE BROTH AND ADD THE SALT AND PEPPER.
- BRING TO A BOIL, THEN LOWER THE HEAT AND SIMMER FOR AN HOUR TO AN HOUR AND A HALF.
- IF YOU WANT TO ADD PASTA, NOW IS THE TIME. COOK PASTA PER INSTRUCTIONS ON THE BOX.
- SERVE WITH A SPRINKLE OF PARMESAN CHEESE ON TOP.

ITALIAN WEDDING SOUP

INGREDIENTS

- MEATBALLS (YOU'LL FIND MY MEATBALL RECIPE ON PAGE 36). YOU WILL JUST NEED TO ROLL THE BALLS VERY SMALL. I MAKE THE BATCH OF MEATBALLS AND ONLY USE HALF AND FREEZE THE OTHER HALF)

* *

THE SOUP

- 1 ONION: DICED
- 2 STALKS CELERY; DICED
- 3 PEELED CARROTS: DICED
- 3 32 OZ CARTONS OF CHICKEN BROTH
- 1 CUP ORZO PASTA
- 2 TABLESPOONS OLIVE OIL
- 2 GARLIC CLOVES; MINCED
- 2 CUPS ESCAROLE; WASHED AND CHOPPED

COOKING PROCESS

- MAKE THE MEATBALLS AND ADD TO A STOCK POT WITH OLIVE OIL.
- COOK MEATBALLS ON MEDIUM HEAT, BROWN ON ALL SIDES (THEY WILL COOK COMPLETELY IN THE SOUP).
- IN A SAUTÉ PAN ADD OLIVE OIL, CARROTS, CELERY, ONIONS AND GARLIC. COOK ON MEDIUM HEAT FOR ABOUT 5 MINUTES.
- ADD THE ESCAROLE TO THAT PAN AND COOK FOR ANOTHER 5 MINUTES.
- TRANSFER ALL THE VEGGIES TO THE POT AND ADD IN THE CHICKEN BROTH.
- ADD SALT AND PEPPER AND BRING TO A BOIL.
- LOWER THE HEAT TO SIMMER FOR 1 HOUR.
- ADD THE ORZO IN AND COOK PER DIRECTIONS ON BOX.
- SERVE WITH A SPRINKLE OF PARMESAN CHEESE.

2

PASTA PERFECTION:

Sauces and Dishes

WHEN YOU COOK WITH LOVE, EVERY MEAL IS A CELEBRATION

SUNDAY SAUCE

SUNDAY'S IN MY KITCHEN, ARE FOR SAUCE!

INGREDIENTS

- OLIVE OIL
- 2 28 OZ CANS TOMATO SAUCE
- 4 6 OZ CANS TOMATO PASTE
- 1 LARGE VIDALIA ONION; MINCED
- 10 CLOVES OF FRESH GARLIC; MINCED
- 1 CUP FRESH BASIL LEAVES
- 4-6 PORK NECK BONES
- 2 TABLESPOONS SALT
- 2 TABLESPOONS PEPPER

WATER TO THIN OUT THE SAUCE AS NEEDED.

COOKING PROCESS

- ADD A COUPLE OF TURNS OF OLIVE OIL TO THE BOTTOM OF A BIG STOCK POT.
- ADD THE NECKBONES TO THE POT AND COOK ON MEDIUM UNTIL BROWNED ON BOTH SIDES.
- ADD IN THE ONION AND GARLIC AND CONTINUE COOKING UNTIL SOFT. ABOUT 5 MINUTES.
- ADD TOMATO SAUCE AND THEN THE TOMATO PASTE.
- FILL EACH CAN OF TOMATO PASTE WITH WATER AND ADD TO THE POT. YOU CAN ADD MORE WATER AS THE SAUCE COOKS TO YOUR DESIRED CONSISTENCY.
- ADD THE SALT, PEPPER AND BASIL.
- SIMMER ON LOW HEAT FOR 2-3 HOURS STIRRING FREQUENTLY.

IF YOU'VE MADE MEATBALLS/BRACIOLE,
THIS IS THE POINT WHERE YOU'D ADD THOSE INTO THE SAUCE.

FRESH TOMATO SAUCE

This is my most favorite sauce
to put over any pasta. The vidalia onion
with the Roma tomatoes gives the sauce
a sweet, yet savory flavor.

INGREDIENTS

- 20 ROMA TOMATOES CUT INTO FOURTHS
- 1/2 CUP OLIVE OIL
- 12 PEELED FRESH WHOLE GARLIC CLOVES
- 1 LARGE VIDALIA ONION; SLICED THIN
- 1 CUP FRESH BASIL
- 2 TEASPOONS SALT
- 2 TEASPOONS PEPPER

You will need either a
food mill or an immersion blender to grind this
down to be a smooth, beautiful
marinara sauce.

COOKING PROCCESS

- HEAT A MEDIUM STOCK POT ON LOW AND POUR HALF OF THE OLIVE OIL INTO THE POT.
- ADD THE TOMATOES, GARLIC, ONION, BASIL, SALT AND PEPPER TO THE POT.
- POUR THE REST OF THE OLIVE OIL OVER THE TOMATO MIXTURE AND SIMMER FOR 2 HOURS, STIRRING FREQUENTLY.
- WHEN SAUCE IS DONE COOKING, USE IMMERSION BLENDER TO PUREE THE SAUCE. YOU MAY WANT TO ADD MORE SALT TO YOUR LIKING. THIS WILL BECOME A SMOOTH MARINARA SAUCE THAT IS LIGHT AND HEALTHY AFTER IT'S BLENDED OR YOU RUN IT THROUGH THE FOOD MILL.

MEDITERRANEAN EGGPLANT AND OLIVE PASTA

INGREDIENTS

- 2 TABLESPOONS OLIVE OIL
- 1 SMALL EGGPLANT(YOU CAN ALSO USE 1 SMALL ZUCCHINI); DICED
- 8 SLICES OF BACON; CHOPPED INTO BITE SIZE PIECES
- 2 TEASPOONS OF FRESH GARLIC; CRUSHED
- 2 CUPS CHERRY TOMATOES; CHOPPED
- 1/4 TEASPOON SALT
- 1/4 TEASPOON PEPPER
- 3 HARD BOILED EGGS; GRATED
- 1 LB PENNE RIGATE PASTA
- 2 TABLESPOONS FRESH BASIL; CHOPPED
- 2 TABLESPOONS GREEN OLIVES; CHOPPED
- GRATED PARMESAN FOR SERVING

COOKING PROCESS

- HEAT THE OLIVE OIL IN A PAN.
- ADD TOMATOES AND THE EGGPLANT. COOK UNTIL SOFT.
- SET ASIDE AND WIPE OUT THE OIL.
- ADD THE CHOPPED BACON TO THE PAN AND COOK ON LOW HEAT UNTIL GOLDEN BROWN.
- STIR THE BACON FREQUENTLY SO IT DOESN'T BURN. (YOU WANT TO KEEP ALL OF THE FAT IN THE PAN.)
- ADD THE GARLIC TO THE BACON.
- COOK FOR 1 MINUTE
- ADD THE EGGPLANT,TOMATOES, OLIVES, SALT AND PEPPER.
- COOK FOR ANOTHER 5 MINUTES TO MELT THE FLAVORS TOGETHER.
- BRING A POT OF SALTED WATER TO A BOIL AND COOK THE PASTA UNTIL IT'S AL DENTE.
- DRAIN THE PASTA, AND DUMP INTO THE SKILLET WITH THE VEGGIES.
- PLATE THE PASTA AND SPRINKLE A HANDFUL OF THE GRATED EGG OVER EACH DISH.
- SERVE WITH A SPRINKLE OF PARMESAN CHEESE OVER THE TOP.

PASTA CARBONARA

A creamy, savory pasta

INGREDIENTS

- 1 LB SPAGHETTI
- 10 OUNCES BACON OR PANCETTA; DICED INTO BITE-SIZE PIECES
- 2 WHOLE EGGS
- 2 EGG YOLKS
- 1/2 CUP GRATED PECORINO ROMANO CHEESE
- 2 TABLESPOONS RESERVED PASTA WATER
- FRESHLY GROUND PEPPER
- 1 CUP FROZEN PEAS; COOKED PER DIRECTIONS ON PACKAGE

COOKING PROCESS

· IN A LARGE SAUTÉ PAN COOK THE PANCETTA OR THE BACON ON MEDIUM HEAT UNTIL CRIPSY
· REMOVE THE MEAT AND SET ASIDE; SAVE ALL OF THE FAT IN THE PAN
· ADD WATER TO A LARGE POT AND BRING TO A BOIL. ADD
THE PASTA AND COOK UNTIL AL DENTE. RESERVE 1/2 CUP OF PASTA WATER AND THEN DRAIN
THE PASTA.
· IN A MEDIUM BOWL WHISK THE EGGS AND EGG YOLKS TOGETHER.
· ADD THE PECORINO ROMANO CHEESE AND 2 TABLESPOONS OF THE RESERVED PASTA WATER.
SET ASIDE..
· ADD THE COOKED PASTA TO THE SAUTE PAN WITH THE BACON FAT AND TOSS FOR 2 MINUTES
ON LOW HEAT. REMOVE FROM HEAT.
· ADD THE EGG/CHEESE MIXTURE, PEAS, THE RESERVED PASTA WATER AND CONTINUE TO TOSS
FOR 2-3 MINUTES.
· SERVE WITH FRESHLY GROUND PEPPER AND ADDITIONAL PECORINO ROMANO CHEESE.

CLASSIC BRACIOLE

Braciole are steak-stuffed rolls
of deliciousness, that cook
in my Sunday sauce for hours.
The sauce is so flavorful after the
braciole cook in it.

INGREDIENTS

- 1 LB THIN SLICED SANDWICH STEAKS
- 1/2 LB SLICED PROSCIUTTO
- 5-6 CLOVES FRESHLY MINCED GARLIC
- 1 CUP PARMESAN CHEESE
- LOTS OF OLIVE OIL
- 1 CUP PLAIN BREADCRUMBS
- 1 TEASPOON SALT
- 1 TEASPOON PEPPER
- 1/4 CUP FRESHLY CHOPPED PARSLEY

COOKING PROCESS

- IN MEDIUM SIZED BOWL COMBINE PARMESAN CHEESE, OLIVE OIL, SALT,
PEPPER,
BREADCRUMBS AND PARSLEY.
(YOU'RE LOOKING FOR A PASTELIKE CONSISTENCY FOR THIS STEP), ADD
OLIVE OIL IN
SLOWLY UNTIL YOU HAVE THAT CONSISTENCY.
SET ASIDE.
- LAY OUT THE STEAKS AND SPOON ON A LAYER OF THE BREADCRUMB
MIXTURE ON TO EACH STEAK. MAKE IT AS THICK OR THIN AS YOU LIKE.
- LAY ONE PIECE OF PROSCIUTTO ON TOP OF THE BREADCRUMB MIXTURE.
- SPRINKLE PARSLEY
ON EACH STEAK.
- ROLL EACH STEAK LIKE A JELLY ROLL AND TIE
WITH KITCHEN TWINE.

- POUR OLIVE OIL INTO THE BOTTOM OF A SAUTÉ PAN, ENOUGH TO COAT
THE
BOTTOM AND ADD IN THE BRACIOLE. BROWN ON ALL
SIDES AND THEN ADD TO SUNDAY
SAUCE TO COOK FULLY.

/30

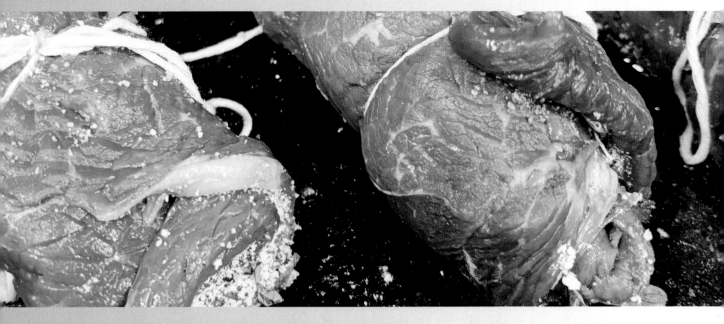

ARANCINI

SICILIAN STUFFED FRIED RICEBALLS

Arancini are a delicacy in my kitchen. I make them every year for Christmas Eve, for our holiday celebration. They are one of my most favorite things to make for our big family.

INGREDIENTS

•THE RICE:

- 5 CUPS CHICKEN STOCK
- 1 TEASPOON SAFFRON THREADS
- 2 CUPS MEDIUM GRAIN RICE
- 3 TABLESPOONS BUTTER
- SALT TO TASTE
- 1/2 CUP FRESHLY GRATED PARMESAN CHEESE
- 1/2 CUP FRESHLY GRATED PECORINO ROMANO CHEESE
- 4 LARGE EGG YOLKS

•THE FILLING:

- TOMATO SAUCE (I USE MY SUNDAY SAUCE AND ADD COOKED GROUND BEEF TO IT)
- 1/2 CUP FROZEN PEAS

•ASSEMBLY:

- 6 LARGE EGG WHITES
- 4 CUPS PLAIN BREADCRUMBS
- FLOUR FOR DREDGING
- 1/2 LB MOZZARELLA OR PROVOLONE CHEESE; SLICED INTO SMALL PIECES
- VEGETABLE OIL FOR DEEP FRYING

COOKING PROCESS:

FOR THE FILLING, I USE
MY SUNDAY SAUCE AND ADD ABOUT 1/2 LB
OF COOKED GROUND CHUCK TO IT.
YOU CAN USE ANY TOMATO SAUCE YOU
CHOOSE. I END UP USING ABOUT 6 CUPS
OF MY SAUCE (GIVE OR TAKE)
I PLACE THE SAUCE IN A SAUCEPAN
AND ADD THE PEAS. SIMMER UNTIL
PEAS ARE SOFT.

TO MAKE THE RICE, BRING THE CHICKEN
STOCK AND THE SAFFRON TO A BOIL IN A
LARGE POT. STIR IN THE RICE, BUTTER AND SALT
TO TASTE.
COVER THE RICE AND SIMMER FOR ABOUT 15-18
MINUTES OR UNTIL THE RICE IS TENDER.
REMOVE THE RICE FROM THE STOVETOP AND ADD
IN THE CHEESES. STIR UNTIL NICELY COMBINED. MOVE THE RICE TO A BIG BOWL.
LET THE RICE COOL AND THEN ADD IN THE EGG YOLKS.
(BE SURE THE RICE ISN'T HOT OR THE EGGS WILL SCRAMBLE AND
YOU DO NOT WANT THAT).

ASSEMBLY:

BEAT THE EGG WHITES UNTIL FOAMY. DUMP A MOUND OF
BREADCRUMBS ON A SHEET OF FOIL, AND DUMP FLOUR
ONTO ANOTHER SHEET OF FOIL. I LIKE TO SET IT UP LIKE AN
ASSEMBLY LINE.

YOU'LL WANT TO DIP YOUR HANDS IN COOL WATER BEFORE
ASSEMBLING EACH RICE BALL, AS THIS WILL PREVENT STICKING.

SCOOP ABOUT 1/4 CUP OF RICE MIXTURE AND PLACE IN
THE PALM OF ONE HAND. POKE A SMALL HOLE IN THE CENTER
OF THE RICE. PRESS ABOUT 1 TABLESPOON OF THE FILLING
INTO THE HOLE AND TOP IT WITH A PIECE OF MOZZARELLA
(OR PROVOLONE). CUP YOUR HAND JUST SLIGHTLY, AND
ADD ANOTHER 1/4 CUP OF RICE MIXTURE OVER THE HOLE.
FORM INTO A BALL CLOSING THE HOLE COMPLETELY. GENTLY
SQUEEZE THE BALL SO IT COMPACTS TOGETHER.

ROLL THE BALL IN FLOUR, DIP IN THE EGG WHITES AND COAT
COMPLETELY AND THEN ROLL THE BALL IN THE BREADCRUMBS.
BE SURE ALL SPOTS ARE COVERED
PLACE EACH RICE BALL ON A RACK UNTIL YOU'RE DONE ROLLING THEM ALL
REFRIGERATE FOR ABOUT AN HOUR.

/33

THE FINAL STEP!

- I use an electric fryer to cook my arancini. It's a 2.9 quart fryer.
- Pour 1 1/2 gallons of vegetable oil into the fryer (I do this in my garage because frying oil stinks... badly).
- Heat fryer to 350 degrees.
- Once the fryer is done heating, drop 4 RICE BALLS in at a time and cook until they're crispy golden brown ~5-6 minutes.
- Set on paper towels as they come out of the fryer to get excess oil off and serve.

RUSTIC ITALIAN BREAD

INGREDIENTS

- 5 CUPS FLOUR
- 2 TBSP OF ACTIVE DRY YEAST
- 2 TABLESPOONS OLIVE OIL
- 3 TEASPOONS KOSHER SALT
- 20 OZ WARM WATER
- 1/4 TEASPOON SUGAR

COOKING PROCESS

- SPRAY A LARGE BOWL WITH OLIVE OIL COOKING SPRAY; SET ASIDE.

- IN STAND MIXER, ADD WATER AND YEAST. MIX TO DISSOLVE YEAST.

- ADD FLOUR, SUGAR, SALT AND OIL.

- MIX UNTIL THE DOUGH COMES OFF THE SIDES OF THE BOWL
- REMOVE DOUGH FROM BOWL AND KNEAD WITH SOME FLOUR FOR A FEW MINUTES.
FORM INTO A BALL AND PUT IT INTO THE BOWL YOU SPRAYED WITH OLIVE OIL COOKING SPRAY.
- COVER WITH PLASTIC WRAP AND A TOWEL. PUT IN A WARM PLACE AND LET IT RISE FOR ONE HOUR.

- PREHEAT OVEN TO 450 DEGREES.
- SET A 13X9 PAN OF WATER ON BOTTOM RACK.
(THIS WILL KEEP THE MOISTURE IN THE OVEN).
- TAKE THE DOUGH OUT OF THE BOWL AND KNEAD AGAIN FOR JUST A MINUTE.
- CUT THE DOUGH IN HALF, MAKING TWO LOAVES. PLACE THE DOUGH FAR ENOUGH APART ON BAKING
SHEETS AND COVER AGAIN WITH THE PLASTIC WRAP AND TOWEL. LET IT RISE AGAIN FOR 30 MINUTES.
- CUT LINES IN THE TOPS OF THE LOAVES WITH A SHARP KNIFE AND PLACE IN HOT OVEN.

BAKE FOR 25 MINUTES

GRAMPA'S FAVORITE MEATBALLS

Whenever my parents are in town, or we are at their house in Florida, my dad always asks me to make my meatballs and I am always happy to do that for him♥

*MAKES ABOUT 25 MEATBALLS

INGREDIENTS

- OLIVE OIL FOR COOKING
- 1 LB GROUND CHUCK
- 1 LB GROUND PORK
- 1 MEDIUM ONION; DICED
- 5 CLOVES FRESH GARLIC; FINELY CHOPPED
- 2 EGGS
- 1 CUP PARMESAN CHEESE
- 2 TEASPOONS SALT
- 2 TEASPOONS PEPPER
- 1/4 CUP FRESHLY CHOPPED PARSLEY

COOKING PROCESS

- COVER THE BOTTOM OF A PAN WITH OLIVE OIL. ADD IN THE ONION AND GARLIC AND SAUTÉ UNTIL TENDER. 5-6 MINUTES.
- COMBINE THE PORK AND BEEF A BOWL.
- ADD THE PARMESAN CHEESE, EGGS, SPICES AND ONION MIXTURE. MIX WELL,
- SCOOP OUT MEAT AND FORM ROUND BALLS.
- COVER THE BOTTOM OF A LARGE PAN WITH OLIVE OIL AND ADD MEATBALLS IN SMALL BATCHES. COOK ON ALL SIDES UNTIL BROWNED. THEN DROP INTO SUNDAY SAUCE AND CONTINUE TO COOK FOR 2-3 HOURS.

JOSEPHINE'S RISOTTO

This risotto is such an amazing side to so many of my dishes. It's so easy and so flavorful. Simple ingredients and delicious flavor.

INGREDIENTS

- 3 CUPS OF MY SUNDAY SAUCE

- 2 CANS OF CHICKEN BROTH

- I CUP WATER

- 2 CUPS LONG GRAIN RICE

- PARMESAN CHEESE

COOKING PROCESS

- PLACE THE TOMATO SAUCE, CHICKEN BROTH AND WATER IN A BIG SAUCE PAN AND BRING TO A BOIL.
- ADD THE RICE AND COOK ON LOW STIRRING FREQUENTLY UNTIL RICE IS TENDER AND HAS ABSORBED MOST OF THE LIQUID.
- TAKE THE RICE OFF THE HEAT.
- TOP WITH GRATED PARMESAN CHEESE AND SERVE.

CANNELLONI WITH GROUND VEAL AND GROUND BEEF

INGREDIENTS

- 2 BOXES CANNELLONI
- TOMATO SAUCE (I USE MY FRESH TOMATO SAUCE ON PAGE 26)
- I LB GROUND VEAL
- I LB GROUND BEEF
- 1/2 LB RICOTTA CHEESE
- 2 EGGS
- I CUP FRESH SPINACH; CHOPPED, STEAMED AND STRAINED
- I CUP GRATED PARMESAN CHEESE
- SALT AND PEPPER
- 1/4 CUP FRESH PARSLEY;CHOPPED
- 2 GARLIC CLOVES;MINCED
- 3 CUPS SHREDDED MOZZARELLA CHEESE
(OR AS MUCH AS YOU LIKE)

COOKING PROCESS

- BROWN BOTH THE VEAL/BEEF IN A PAN; SET ASIDE TO LET COOL.
- PREHEAT OVEN TO 350 DEGREES.
- IN A MEDIUM BOWL MIX THE RICOTTA, PARMESAN CHEESE, EGGS, SPINACH, SALT, PEPPER, GARLIC AND PARSLEY.
- ADD IN THE GROUND MEATS AND MIX WELL.
- BOIL WATER IN A LARGE POT AND ADD THE CANNELLONI AND COOK FOR ABOUT 5 MINUTES (YOU DON'T WANT THEM TOO SOFT).
- DRAIN AND COOL FOR A FEW MINUTES.
- ADD THE MEAT MIXTURE TO A PIPING BAG (I USE A ZIPLOC AND CUT THE TIP) AND FILL EACH CANNELLONI.
- IN A 13X9 BAKING PAN SPREAD TOMATO SAUCE ON THE BOTTOM OF THE PAN.
- ADD EACH CANNELLONI AS YOU FILL THEM.
- CONTINUE THE PROCESS UNTIL THE PAN IS FULL.
- TOP WITH A GENEROUS AMOUNT OF SAUCE.
- SPRINKLE MOZZARELLA CHEESE ON TOP.
- BAKE AT 350 DEGREES COVERED WITH FOIL FOR 30 MINUTES.
- REMOVE FOIL AND COOK 5 MORE MINUTES.
- TOP WITH SPRINKLED PARMESAN CHEESE AND SERVE.

3

SAVORY SIDES

COOKING WITH LOVE IS THE JOURNEY
TO A JOYFUL HEART

BACKYARD BBQ BEANS

The perfect side for a backyard BBQ.
This recipe is something I get asked to make
all summer long.

INGREDIENTS

· 2 15 OZ CANS PORK & BEANS
(IN TOMATO SAUCE)
· 1/2 LB GROUND BEEF
· 1/2 CUP BARBECUE SAUCE
· 1/2 CUP BROWN SUGAR

COOKING PROCESS

PREHEAT OVEN TO 350 DEGREES
· BROWN THE GROUND BEEF
AND DRAIN THE FAT.
· IN A SHALLOW BAKING PAN
COMBINE THE PORK AND BEANS,
GROUND BEEF, BARBECUE SAUCE
AND BROWN SUGAR.
· MIX WELL AND THEN SPREAD
EVENLY IN PAN.
· SPRINKLE A BIT MORE BROWN SUGAR
AND A LITTLE BIT MORE BARBECUE SAUCE
ON TOP.
· BAKE AT 350 DEGREES FOR 30 MINUTES

/40

GRILLED BREADED EGGPLANT

ZIO ANGELO'S RECIPE

INGREDIENTS
- 1 EGGPLANT
(IF YOU CAN FIND SICILIAN
EGGPLANT, USE THAT!)
- PLAIN BREAD CRUMBS
- OLIVE OIL
- SALT AND PEPPER
TO TASTE

COOKING PROCESS
- WASH EGGPLANT AND PAT DRY.
- CUT THE EGGPLANT
INTO 1/2 INCH SLICES.
- GET TWO BOWLS READY. ONE
FOR BREADCRUMBS
AND ONE FOR OLIVE OIL.
- HEAT THE GRILL
- DIP EACH SLICE OF EGGPLANT
INTO OLIVE OIL AND THEN INTO
BREADCRUMBS. BE SURE TO
COAT VERY WELL WITH BOTH
STEPS.
- PLACE ON HEATED GRILL AND
COOK UNTIL SOFT.
APPROXIMATELY
8 MINUTES PER SIDE.

/41

ZUCCHINI FRITTERS

These fritters are something I make all year round. I freeze all of my grated zucchini from my summer garden so we can enjoy them throughout every season.

INGREDIENTS

- 2 CUPS GRATED ZUCCHINI; BE SURE TO SQUEEZE OUT ANY EXCESS WATER(SKIN ON)
- 1 CUP PLAIN PANKO BREADCRUMBS
- 2 EGGS
- 1/4 CUP GRATED PARMESAN CHEESE
- 2 GARLIC CLOVES; MINCED
- AVOCADO OIL FOR FRYING

COOKING PROCESS

- GRATE ZUCCHINI ON BOX GRATER AND SQUEEZE OUT ALL OF THE WATER.
- ADD ZUCCHINI AND ALL OTHER INGREDIENTS TO A BOWL AND MIX WELL.
- HEAT THE AVOCADO OIL IN A SKILLET AND USE A SMALL BAKING SCOOP TO FORM THE FRITTERS. FLATTEN THEM LIKE A SMALL PANCAKE.
- LAY EACH FRITTER IN THE PAN AND COOK 6-7 MINUTES ON EACH SIDE OR UNTIL GOLDEN BROWN.
- TRANSFER TO A PAPER TOWEL LINED DISH SO EXCESS OIL IS SOAKED UP.

GRILLED ZUCCHINI WITH SHAVED PECORINO ROMANO

THERE IS NOTHING BETTER THAN HOME GROWN ZUCCHINI.

INGREDIENTS

- 1 LARGE ZUCCHINI
- 1/4 CUP SHAVED PECORINO ROMANO CHEESE
- OLIVE OIL
- SALT & PEPPER TO TASTE
- 1/2 TEASPOON PAPRIKA

COOKING PROCESS

- SLICE THE ZUCCHINI INTO LONG 1 in. WIDE PIECES
- IN A SHALLOW BOWL, ADD ZUCCHINI AND A SPLASH OF OLIVE OIL AND THE SPICES.
- SPRAY YOUR COOK TOP GRILL WITH OLIVE OIL COOKING SPRAY AND HEAT ON LOW.
- ADD THE ZUCCHINI SLICES IN AND COOK ON MEDIUM UNTIL TENDER AND NICE GRILL LINES APPEAR. ABOUT 5 MINUTES PER SIDE.
- SPRINKLE THE CHEESE OVER THE COOKED ZUCCHINI AND SERVE.

ARTICHOKE CASSEROLE

INGREDIENTS

- 1 CAN QUARTERED ARTICHOKES; DRAINED
- 1 SMALL CAN FRENCH STYLE GREEN BEANS; DRAINED
- 2 FRESH GARLIC CLOVES; MINCED
- 4 TABLESPOONS OLIVE OIL + 2 TABLESPOONS FOE DRIZZLE ON TOP
- 1 CUP PLAIN BREADCRUMBS + A HANDFUL FOR TOPPING
- 1 CUP PARMESAN CHEESE
- 1 TEASPOON SALT
- 1 TEASPOON PEPPER

COOKING PROCESS

- PREHEAT OVEN TO 350 DEGREES.
- SPRAY 9x9 PAN WITH OLIVE OIL COOKING SPRAY.
- IN A MEDIUM SIZE BOWL COMBINE ARTICHOKES, BEANS, PARMESAN CHEESE, BREADCRUMBS, 3 TABLESPOONS OLIVE OIL, GARLIC , SALT AND PEPPER.
- SPREAD INTO THE PAN AND SPRINKLE A HANDFUL OF BREADCRUMBS OVER THE TOP AND DRIZZLE OF OLIVE OIL.
- BAKE AT 350 DEGREES FOR 30 MINUTES.

ROASTED ASPARAGUS
WITH BALSAMIC DRIZZLE

INGREDIENTS

- 1 BUNCH FRESH ASPARAGUS
- 1 TEASPOON KOSHER SALT
- 2 TABLESPOONS OLIVE OIL
- BALSAMIC GLAZE

COOKING PROCESS

- WASH AND PAT DRY ASPARAGUS.
- PREHEAT OVEN TO 400 DEGREES.
- TOSS ASPARAGUS WITH OLIVE OIL AND SALT IN A SMALL BOWL.
- SPRAY A BAKING SHEET WITH OLIVE OIL COOKING SPRAY.
- LAY THE ASPARAGUS ON THE PAN AND ROAST FOR 10 MINUTES OR UNTIL TENDER.
- DRIZZLE BALSAMIC GLAZE AND SERVE

/45

EASY PEASY PEAS WITH ONIONS

INGREDIENTS

- 1 12 OZ BAG FROZEN SWEET PEAS
- 4 TABLESPOONS OLIVE OIL
- 1 SMALL ONION; DICED
- 1 TEASPOON SALT
- 1 TEASPOON PEPPER

COOKING PROCESS

- IN A MEDIUM SIZED SAUCEPAN ADD PEAS, ONION, OLIVE OIL, SALT & PEPPER.
- TURN HEAT ON LOW.
- MIX WELL AND THEN COVER
- SIMMER ON VERY LOW FLAME UNTIL PEAS AND ONIONS ARE SOFT AND THE PEAS ARE A BIT CARAMELIZED.
- STIR FREQUENTLY AND COOK ABOUT 15 MINUTES.

STUFFED ARTICHOKES

INGREDIENTS

- 4 LARGE ARTICHOKES
- 2 CUPS PLAIN BREADCRUMBS
- 2 CUPS GRATED PECORINO ROMANO CHEESE
- 3 CLOVES GARLIC; MINCED
- 2 TEASPOONS FRESH PARSLEY; CHOPPED
- 4 TBS OLIVE OIL
- 1 LEMON QUARTERED
- SALT & PEPPER TO TASTE

COOKING PROCESS

PREHEAT OVEN TO 375° DEGREES.
~ TO PREPARE ARTICHOKES, CUT ONE INCH OFF THE TOP.
THEN CUT OFF STEMS SO ARTICHOKES SIT FLAT.
~ SNIP THE TIPS OF THE LEAVES AND RUB HALF OF A LEMON OVER THE WHOLE ARTICHOKE TO PREVENT FROM BURNING.
~ MIX TOGETHER BREADCRUMBS, CHEESE, GARLIC, PARSLEY, SALT, PEPPER AND OLIVE OIL IN A BOWL.
~ OPEN ARTICHOKES BY GENTLY PULLING LEAVES APART. STUFF THE ARTICHOKES WITH THE BREADCRUMB MIXTURE. PACKING THE LEAVES NICE
AND THICK.
~ PLACE THE ARTICHOKES IN A SMALL BAKING DISH SO THEY ARE TIGHTLY NESTLED. POUR ABOUT AN INCH OF WATER ON THE BOTTOM OF THE PAN.
~ DRIZZLE OLIVE OIL OVER THE TOPS OF ARTICHOKES AND SQUEEZE A HALF A LEMON OVER.
~ COVER THE BAKING DISH WITH FOIL AND BAKE FOR ONE HOUR AND FIFTEEN MINUTES.
~ REMOVE THE FOIL AND BAKE FOR ANOTHER 10 MINUTES.

BACON-INFUSED GREEN BEAN SAUTÉ

If I had to pick a favorite side dish, this is the one. When I make this for my family, I have to triple the recipe because we all love it so much.

INGREDIENTS

- 1 LB FRESHLY TRIMMED, STEAMED STRING BEANS (OR 4 CANS CUT GREEN BEANS. BE SURE TO DRAIN IF YOU'RE USING CANS)
- 1/2 LB BACON; CHOPPED INTO BITE-SIZE PIECES
- 2 TABLESPOONS GRANULATED ONION
- 1 TEASPOON SALT
- 1/2 TEASPOON PEPPER

COOKING PROCESS

- SAUTÉ BACON ON LOW HEAT UNTIL GOLDEN BROWN. BE SURE TO COOK VERY SLOWLY AND EVENLY TO KEEP ALL OF THE DRIPPINGS - STIRRING EVERY FEW MINUTES.
- ADD THE STRING BEANS TO THE BACON AND DRIPPINGS AND SPRINKLE THE GRANULATED ONION, SALT AND PEPPER ON.
- COOK FOR 5-10 MINUTES ON LOW TO MELT THE FLAVORS TOGETHER.

/48

4

POTATO SIDEKICKS

COOKING FOR FAMILY AND
FRIENDS
IS THE MOST SINCERE FORM OF
LOVE

/49

SWEET POTATO MEDLEY

INGREDIENTS

- 2 LARGE SWEET POTATOES PEELED AND CUT INTO BITE-SIZE PIECES
- 2 LARGE YELLOW POTATOES; PEELED AND CUT INTO BITE-SIZE PIECES
- I LARGE VIDALIA ONION; SLICED THIN
- 2 TABLESPOONS OLIVE OIL
- 3 TABLESPOONS BUTTER
- I/2 TEASPOON SALT
- I/2 TEASPOON PEPPER

I absolutely love these potatoes. The onion makes the flavor of the sweet potatoes pop and the yellow potato balances out the flavor of the whole dish.

COOKING PROCESS

- PLACE THE CUT POTATOES AND ONION INTO A LARGE SAUTÉ PAN.
- POUR THE OLIVE OIL OVER, AND ADD THE BUTTER.
- SPRINKLE WITH SALT AND GIVE IT A GOOD TOSS.
- COVER AND COOK ON LOW HEAT. STIR FREQUENTLY UNTIL POTATOES ARE TENDER.

/50

GOLDEN ROASTED CRISPY POTATOES

INGREDIENTS

- 4 MEDIUM YELLOW POTATOES;SKIN ON (YOU CAN USE RED POTATOES AS WELL)
- 3 TABLESPOONS OLIVE OIL
- 1/2 STICK BUTTER
- 2-3 TABLESPOONS FRESH CHOPPED PARSLEY
- 4 FRESH GARLIC CLOVES;CRUSHED (I USE A GARLIC PRESS)
- SALT AND PEPPER TO TASTE

COOKING PROCESS

- IN A LARGE SAUCEPAN ADD WHOLE POTATOES AND COVER WITH WATER
- COOK ON MEDIUM HEAT UNTIL JUST FORK TENDER. (YOU DON'T WANT THEM TO SOFT)
- DRAIN WATER AND CUT POTATOES INTO BITE-SIZE CHUNKS.
- ADD CUT POTATOES TO A SAUTÉ PAN
- ADD THE OLIVE OIL, BUTTER, GARLIC, PARSLEY, SALT AND PEPPER.MIX WELL.
- SIMMER ON LOW HEAT UNTIL POTATOES ARE TENDER AND SLIGHTLY BROWNED.

These potatoes are so hearty and satisfying. They're the perfect side to any meal!

/51

5

VIBRANT FRESH SALADS

IN EVERY FAMILY DISH, THERE IS A STORY OF TRADITION AND LOVE

/52

ASIAN CRISPY SUMMER SALAD

INGREDIENTS

- 1 PACKAGE OF RAMEN NOODLES (DISCARD THE FLAVOR PACKET)
- 1 HEAD OF ROMAINE LETTUCE: CHOPPED
- 1 CUP SLICED ALMONDS

DRESSING

- 1/2 CUP APPLE CIDER VINEGAR
- 2 TABLESPOONS SOY SAUCE
- 1/4 CUP OLIVE OIL
- 1 CUP SUGAR
- WHISK TOGETHER AND SET ASIDE.

COOKING PROCESS

PREHEAT OVEN TO 350 DEGREES

- TAKE THE RAMEN NOODLES AMD GENTLY BREAK INTO SMALL PIECES. PLACE THE RAMEN NOODLES ON COOKING SHEET AND PLACE THE SLICED ALMONDS ON ANOTHER COOKING SHEET.
- TOAST UNTIL BOTH ARE BROWNED. ABOUT 10 MINUTES DEPENDING ON YOUR OVEN.
- WHEN TOASTED REMOVE FROM OVEN AND SET ASIDE.
- CHOP THE ROMAINE AND ADD TO A BOWL.
- ADD THE TOASTED RAMEN AND ALMONDS TO THE BOWL OF ROMAINE AND POUR DRESSING OVER .

/53

Maddie's Summer Salad

This is a summer salad that my niece Maddie absolutely loves. Everything in it is homegrown from my garden. Forgive me on this one...You're going to have to trust me on the measurements. It's all about the amount of "shakes" and "turns".

INGREDIENTS

- 1 RED ONION; SLICED THIN
- 4 YELLOW POTATOES: PEELED & CUT INTO BITE-SIZE PIECES
- 1 LB FRESH STRING BEANS; TRIMMED AND STEAMED
- 2 LARGE HEIRLOOM TOMATOES; CUT INTO CHUNKS
- OLIVE OIL (3-4 TURNS AROUND YOUR BOWL)
- RED WINE VINEGAR (8 SHAKES AROUND YOUR BOWL)
- SALT AND PEPPER TO TASTE
- 2 TABLESPOONS DRIED OREGANO
- 2 TABLESPOONS FRESH CHOPPED BASIL

COOKING PROCESS

- PEEL POTATOES AND BOIL UNTIL FORK TENDER 10-15 MINUTES .
- DRAIN AND ADD TO A BIG BOWL.
- LET COOL.
- ADD THE STEAMED STRING BEANS, ONION AND TOMATOES.
- TAKE YOUR OLIVE OIL AND MAKE 3- 4 GOOD TURNS AROUND THE BOWL.
- TAKE THE VINEGAR AND SHAKE ABOUT 8 TIMES AROUND THE BOWL.
- ADD THE BASIL, OREGANO AND SALT AND PEPPER TO TASTE.
- MIX THOROUGHLY AND ADD IN MORE OF ANYTHING THAT YOU THINK IT NEEDS. (A LOT OF TIMES I END UP ADDING SALT AND EXTRA OLIVE OIL.)

MY ITALIAN GRANDMOTHER'S GERMAN POTATO SALAD

INGREDIENTS

- 5 LBS IDAHO POTATOES
- 1 LB BACON; CHOPPED INTO SMALL PIECES
- 1 YELLOW ONION; DICED
- 4-5 STALKS CELERY; DICED
- 3 TABLESPOONS VEGETABLE OIL
- 1 CUP DISTILLED WHITE VINEGAR
- 1-2 TABLESPOONS SUGAR
- 5 HARD BOILED EGGS; CHOPPED INTO SMALL PIECES
- 2 TEASPOONS FRESH CHOPPED PARSLEY

SALT AND PEPPER TO TASTE

This potato salad is the epitome of HOME to me. I have no idea where my grandmother got this recipe, but it's a fan favorite for sure. It's a lot of steps, but worth every one.

/55

COOKING PROCESS

- IN A BIG STOCKPOT ADD ALL 5 LBS OF POTATOES. SKIN ON.
- COVER COMPLETELY WITH WATER AND COOK ON MEDIUM HEAT, UNTIL JUST FORK TENDER. YOU WANT TO WATCH SO THEY'RE NOT TOO SOFT. THIS CAN TAKE UP TO AN HOUR.
- SET POTATOES ASIDE WHEN DONE COOKING TO COOL COMPLETELY. THEY NEED TO BE COOL TO PEEL.
- ADD BACON TO A LARGE SAUTÉ PAN AND COOK VERY SLOWLY ON LOW HEAT UNTIL BACON IS VERY GOLDEN. STIRRING OFTEN SO THE BACON COOKS EVENLY. (YOU WILL BE SAVING ALL OF THE BACON DRIPPINGS)
- WHILE BACON IS COOKING, ADD THE VEGETABLE OIL TO ANOTHER SAUTÉ PAN AND COOK THE ONION AND CELERY TOGETHER IN THE SAME PAN. YOU MAY NEED TO ADD MORE OIL AS YOU COOK. IT NEEDS TO STAY MOIST. COOK UNTIL TENDER ON LOW/MEDIUM HEAT. YOU WANT THIS MIXTURE TO GET A LITTLE BROWN GLAZE, BUT NOT BE BURNT.

- WHEN THE BACON IS DONE COOKING,
SET ASIDE AND SAVE THE DRIPPINGS.
(THE DRIPPINGS ARE WHAT MAKES THIS
DISH TASTE SO DELISH!)
- AFTER THE CELERY/ONION IS DONE COOKING
ADD THEM TO THE PAN WITH THE BACON/DRIPPINGS.
- ADD THE VINEGAR AND THE SUGAR.
- SIMMER THAT ALL FOR 5 MINUTES ON LOW HEAT.

- MOVE OVER TO THE COOLED POTATOES WHILE YOU
HAVE THE BACON MIXTURE ON THE STOVE TOP.
- WITH YOUR HANDS PEEL EACH POTATO. (DON'T ASK ME
WHY WE
PEEL WITH OUR HANDS AFTER THEY'RE COOKED...
ITS JUST WHAT I WAS TAUGHT.)
- AFTER POTATOES ARE PEELED USE A PAIRING KNIFE
TO CUT INTO BITE-SIZE PIECES.
- ADD CUT POTATOES TO A LARGE OVEN SAFE BOWL.
- POUR THE ENTIRE PAN OF BACON, CELERY, ONION
INTO THE BOWL OF POTATOES.
- POUR THE CHOPPED HARD BOILED EGGS ON TOP AND
SALT AND PEPPER TO TASTE.
- TOSS IT ALL TOGETHER AND THEN KEEP
IN A WARM OVEN UNTIL READY TO SERVE.

Family cooking is not just about
feeding loved ones;
it's about nourishing
the bonds that make us whole.

MINTY WATERMELON SALAD

<u>INGREDIENTS</u>

- 1/2 FRESH WATERMELON; CUT INTO BITE-SIZE PIECES
- 1/4 TEASPOON KOSHER SALT
- THE JUICE OF HALF A LIME
- 1/4 CUP FRESH MINT; CHOPPED FINELY
- CRUMBLED FETA CHEESE IF YOU DESIRE

(I USE 1/4 CUP SHAVED PECORINO ROMANO CHEESE

INSTEAD OF FETA)

- A DRIZZLE OF HONEY ON TOP

~PLACE ALL INGREDIENTS INTO A BOWL

~ MIX WELL

~ DRIZZLE THE HONEY AND SERVE

One of the most refreshing salads I make! It is a must

have for summertime!

/58

MIRANDA'S LEMONY SALAD WITH SHAVED PECORINO

INGREDIENTS

- 1 PACKAGE OF ROMAINE HEARTS
- 10-12 GRAPE TOMATOES SLICED THIN
- 3/4 CUP OF SHAVED PECORINO ROMANO CHEESE
  (WE LIKE A LOT OF CHEESE)
- HIMALAYIAN SEA SALT
- THE JUICE OF HALF A LEMON
- 2 TURNS OF OLIVE OIL
- PLACE THE LETTUCE INTO A MEDIUM BOWL
- ADD THE SHAVED PECORINO CHEESE (I USE
  A BOX GRATER TO SHAVE MINE)
- ADD THE SLICED TOMATOES
- GIVE THE BOWL 2-3 TURNS OF OLIVE OIL
- SQUEEZE THE LEMON JUICE
- ADD THE SALT TO YOUR TASTE. I GRIND ABOUT
  3-4 TIMES
- TOSS TOGETHER AND SERVE

This is my sweet daughter-in-law, Miranda's favorite salad. It's the simplest, freshest, most delicious salad to complement with dinner or just have by itself!

/59

6

SWEET TEMPTATIONS

EVERY FAMILY MEAL IS A CHAPTER IN OUR LOVE STORY

CHRISTOPHER'S ITALIAN LEMON DROP COOKIES

These lemon drop cookies are my youngest son's favorite. He loves them so much he even eats them unfrosted!

INGREDIENTS

- 1/2 CUP SUGAR
- 1/4 CUP VEGETABLE SHORTENING
- 3 LARGE EGGS
- 1 1/2 TEASPOONS LEMON EXTRACT
- 2 CUPS FLOUR
- 1 1/2 TEASPOONS BAKING POWDER
- 1/8 TEASPOON SALT

FROSTING

- 1/2 CUP CONFECTIONERS SUGAR
- 1 TABLESPOON WATER
- 2-3 DROPS OF LEMON EXTRACT
(CONSISTENCY SHOULD BE
ON THE THICKER SIDE. BUT IF YOU
PREFER
IT THINNER, ADD LESS WATER)

COOKING PROCESS

- PREHEAT OVEN TO 350 DEGREES
- CREAM TOGETHER SUGAR & SHORTENING.
- ADD THE EGGS AND LEMON EXTRACT AND BEAT WELL.
- BEAT THE FLOUR IN SLOWLY, BAKING POWDER AND SALT.
- DOUGH SHOULD BE A BIT STICKY YET SOFT
- SCOOP OUT A TEASPOON SIZE AND DROP ONTO PARCHMENT LINED BAKING SHEET.
- PLACE THEM ABOUT 2" APART
- BAKE FOR 10-12 MINUTES
THE BOTTOMS SHOULD BE JUST SLIGHTLY BROWNED
- ALLOW COOKIES TO COOL AND THEN FROST

MR. VALENTI'S SNICKERDOODLES

*MAKES ABOUT 3 DOZEN COOKIES

INGREDIENTS

- 1 CUP SALTED BUTTER
- 1 1/3 CUP GRANULATED SUGAR
- 1/3 CUP BROWN SUGAR
- 2 LARGE EGGS
- 3 TEASPOONS VANILLA EXTRACT
- 3 1/4 CUPS FLOUR
- 1 TEASPOON BAKING SODA
- 3/4 TEASPOON KOSHER SALT
- 1 1/2 TEASPOONS CREAM OF TARTAR

FOR ROLLING

- 1/3 CUP GRANULATED SUGAR
- 1 1/2 TABLESPOONS CINNAMON

COOKING PROCESS

PREHEAT OVEN TO 350 DEGREES

- IN A STAND MIXER, CREAM THE BUTTER FOR A FEW MINUTES UNTIL SMOOTH.
- ADD IN BOTH SUGARS AND BEAT UNTIL CREAMY.
- ADD EGGS AND VANILLA AND BEAT UNTIL SMOOTH.
- ADD THE DRY INGREDIENTS AND CONTINUE MIXING UNTIL THE FLOUR IS NO LONGER VISIBLE OR STREAKY.

- USING A 3/4" COOKIE SCOOP TO FORM DOUGH BALLS, ROLL THE BALLS INTO THE CINNAMON/SUGAR MIXTURE.
- PLACE EACH BALL ON PARCHMENT LINED BAKING SHEET ABOUT 2" APART.
- COOK FOR 9-11 MINUTES. YOU WANT THEM SLIGHTLY UNDERCOOKED.
- LET THEM COOL ON THE BAKING SHEET FOR 5 MINUTES AND THEN TRANSFER TO A COOLING RACK.

OATMEAL CHOCOLATE CHIP COOKIES

*MAKES ABOUT 2 DOZEN COOKIES

INGREDIENTS

- 2 1/2 CUPS ROLLED OATS
- 2 CUPS FLOUR
- 1/2 CUP GRANULATED SUGAR
- 1 CUP BROWN SUGAR
- 1 TEASPOON SALT
- 1 CUP CANOLA OIL
- 2 LARGE EGGS
- 1 TEASPOON BAKING SODA
- 5 TEASPOONS VANILLA
(YES! FIVE!)
- 1 1/2 TEASPOONS CINNAMON
- 1 12 OZ PACKAGE SEMI SWEET
CHOCOLATE CHIPS
*OPTIONAL ADD
1/2 CUP CHOPPED PECANS

COOKING PROCESS

- PREHEAT OVEN TO 350 DEGREES
- COMBINE ALL INGREDIENTS AND MIX WELL
- SHAPE INTO ONE TABLESPOON SIZED BALLS
- BAKE FOR 10-12 MINUTES UNTIL OUTER EDGES
ARE LIGHTLY BROWNED. YOU WANT THEM TO COME
OUT GOOEY.
I KEEP THEM ON THE PAN TO COOL FOR 5 MINUTES
AND THEN TRANSFER TO A RACK.

These cookies are so yummy and super quick to make. I love a recipe that I can throw all of the ingredients right into the bowl and mix!

NONNA'S BISCOTTI

*Makes about 2 dozen cookies

INGREDIENTS

- 1/4 CUP CANDIED CHERRIES
- 3 LARGE EGGS
- 1 1/2 TABLESPOONS VANILLA
- 3/4 CUP SUGAR
- 3/4 CUP CANOLA OIL
- 2 3/4 CUPS FLOUR
- 2 TEASPOONS BAKING POWDER
- 1/4 CUP CHOPPED PECANS (OR YOUR CHOICE OF NUTS)

COOKING PROCESS

- PREHEAT OVEN TO 350 DEGREES
- WHISK THE EGGS, SUGAR, VANILLA AND OIL TOGETHER IN A BOWL.
- STIR IN THE FLOUR AND THE BAKING POWDER.
- MIX WELL. THE DOUGH SHOULD BE SOFT AND NOT TOO STICKY.
- LINE A BAKING SHEET WITH PARCHMENT PAPER.
- SPLIT THE DOUGH INTO 2 LOAVES AND PLACE EACH LOAF ON THE PAN
- SHAPE THEM INTO LOAVES THAT ARE ABOUT 3-4" WIDE AND 9-10" LONG.
- BAKE FOR 20 MINUTES.
- TAKE OUT OF THE OVEN AND SLICE EACH LOAF INTO ONE INCH DIAGONAL SLICES.
- PUT THOSE SLICES BACK INTO THE OVEN AND COOK FOR 5 MINUTES ON EACH SIDE.

These biscotti are a delectable rendition of my mother-in-law's recipe. I promise, you will not find biscotti that are as delicate and tasty as these!

ORANGE RICOTTA OLIVE OIL CAKE WITH LEMON GLAZE

This cake is the perfect addition to any dessert table. It is something I have always had on hand for coffee on the patio. And... it's gluten/dairy free!

INGREDIENTS

- 3 EGGS
- 3/4 CUP DAIRY FREE RICOTTA CHEESE
- 1/4 CUP OLIVE OIL
- 1 1/4 TEASPOONS VANILLA EXTRACT
- 3/4 CUP GRANULATED SUGAR
- 2 TABLESPOONS ORANGE ZEST
- 1/2 CUP FRESHLY SQUEEZED ORANGE JUICE
- 1 3/4 CUPS GLUTEN FREE FLOUR
- 1/2 TEASPOON KOSHER SALT
- 2 TEASPOONS BAKING POWDER
- 1/2 TEASPOON BAKING SODA

LEMON GLAZE

- 1/4 CUP LEMON JUICE
- 2 CUPS CONFECTIONERS SUGAR
- 1/8 TEASPOON WATER
- PINCH OF SALT

COOKING PROCESS

PREHEAT OVEN TO 350 DEGREES
- GREASE ONE LOAF PAN WITH NON STICK COOKING SPRAY.
- LINE THE PAN WITH PARCHMENT PAPER SO YOU WILL BE ABLE TO LIFT THE CAKE OUT OF THE PAN EASILY.
- IN A LARGE BOWL, WHISK TOGETHER THE EGGS AND THE RICOTTA CHEESE UNTIL WELL BLENDED.
- ADD THE OLIVE OIL, VANILLA, SUGAR, ORANGE ZEST, ORANGE JUICE AND WHISK AGAIN.
- ADD THE FLOUR, SALT, BAKING POWDER AND BAKING SODA.
- WHISK UNTIL THERE ARE NO VISIBLE TRACES OF FLOUR. THE BATTER WILL BE LUMPY, BUT DON'T FRET.
- POUR THE BATTER INTO THE GREASED PAN AND BAKE 50-55 MINUTES OR UNTIL A TOOTHPICK POKED IN CENTER COMES OUT CLEAN.
- REMOVE THE CAKE AND LET IT COOL FOR A MINIMUM OF 20 MINUTES IN THE PAN BEFORE MOVING ONTO A WIRE RACK.
- WHILE THE CAKE COOLS, MAKE THE LEMON GLAZE IN A SMALL BOWL.
- POUR THE GLAZE OVER THE COOLED CAKE AND SERVE.

GRAMMIE'S CHEESECAKE

This is the best cheesecake you will ever have. Period. This is my mom's recipe that everyone begs her to make for every holiday.

INGREDIENTS

PREHEAT OVEN TO 350 DEGREES
- 3 8 OZ PACKAGES CREAM CHEESE (ROOM TEMPERATURE)
- 3 EGGS (ROOM TEMPERATURE)
- I TEASPOON VANILLA
- I CUP SUGAR

CRUST

- 1 1/3 CUPS CRUSHED GRAHAM CRACKERS
- 4 TABLESPOONS MELTED MARGARINE
- 2 TABLESPOONS SUGAR
- CRUSH THE GRAHAM CRACKERS IN A FOOD PROCESSOR.
- IN A LARGE BOWL MIX TOGETHER ALL CRUST INGREDIENTS. GRAHAM CRACKERS WILL BE MOIST.
- BLEND WELL AND PRESS INTO THE BOTTOM OF A 9" SPRING FORM PAN.

COOKING PROCESS

- BEAT CREAM CHEESE WELL.
- ADD EGGS ONE AT A TIME.
- ADD SUGAR A LITTLE AT A TIME; BLEND WELL
- ADD VANILLA, BLEND WELL.
- POUR MIXTURE ONTO CRUST AND BAKE AT 350 DEGREES FOR 25-30 MINUTES.
- LET COOL FOR AT LEAST 30 MINUTES ON COUNTER AND THEN REFRIGERATE FOR ANOTHER 30 MINUTES.
- IT MUST BE COOLED COMPLETELY BEFORE YOU ADD THE SOUR CREAM TOPPING.

SOUR CREAM TOPPING

- 16 OZ SOUR CREAM
- I TEASPOON VANILLA
- 3 TABLESPOONS SUGAR BLEND WELL
- SPOON ON (DO NOT POUR!) SOUR CREAM MIXTURE ONTO COOLED CHEESECAKE.
- SPREAD EVENLY WITH A RUBBER SPATULA.
- BAKE 10 MINUTES AT 350 DEGREES.
- COOL FOR 30 MINUTES.
- KEEP IN REFRIGERATOR FOR MINIMUM OF 24 HOURS BEFORE SLICING.

AMAZING APPLE PIE

This is my quick and easy apple pie
that doesn't ever disappoint.

INGREDIENTS

- 6 HONEY CRISP APPLES PEELED, CORED, AND THINLY SLICED
- 3/4 CUP GRANULATED SUGAR
- 2 TABLESPOONS FLOUR
- 1 TABLESPOON LEMON JUICE
- 2 TEASPOONS GROUND CINNAMON
- 1/4 TEASPOON SALT
- 2 PIE CRUSTS (YES … I USE STORE BOUGHT, THIS IS THE ONE AREA I DON'T MIND STORE BOUGHT)

COOKING PROCESS

- PREHEAT OVEN TO 425 DEGREES
- PLACE ONE PIE CRUST INTO THE BOTTOM OF A 9" PIE DISH.
- PRESS AGAINST THE SIDES AND BOTTOM FIRMLY,
- IN A LARGE BOWL ADD ALL INGREDIENTS AND MIX WELL.
- LAY THE SECOND PIE CRUST OVER THE TOP AND PRESS THE EDGES TOGETHER.
- CUT SLITS ON THE TOP OF PIE.
- BAKE FOR 45-50 MINUTES UNTIL TOP IS LIGHTLY BROWNED.
- LET COOL FOR 2 HOURS BEFORE SLICING.

67

ACKNOWLEDGEMENTS

TO THE ONES WHO LOVE ME... YOUR ENCOURAGEMENT TO WRITE THIS COOKBOOK
HAS GIVEN ME LIFE.

MY BOYS AND MY DAUGHTER IN LAW... YOU ARE MY WHOLE HEART AND MY
EVERY BREATH. YOU ARE THE REASON I DO WHAT I DO, EVERY SINGLE DAY.
PLEASE KEEP COMING HOME TO EAT.

TO MY PARENTS WHO GAVE ME THE GREATEST EXAMPLE OF WHAT FAMILY
SHOULD LOOK LIKE. YOU HAVE ALWAYS MADE ME FEEL LIKE I COULD CONQUER
THE WORLD .... I LOVE YOU SO, SO MUCH.

MY BESTEST BESTIE, WITHOUT YOUR ENCOURAGEMENT AND SIDELINE CHEERING,
THIS COOKBOOK WOULDN'T HAVE BEEN A THOUGHT. THANK YOU FOR LOVING MY
FOOD AND ME.

TO THE GUY NEXT DOOR, (HE KNOWS WHO HE IS), YOU HAVE MY HEARTFELT
APPRECIATION FOR ALL OF THE COOKING WE'VE DONE TOGETHER. THANK YOU
FOR NOT MAKING ME EAT THINGS I HATE, AND FOR MAKING RECIPES THAT MAKE
ME HAPPY.

TO MY NIECE WHO COMES HOME AND ASKS ME TO MAKE HER FAVORITES...YOU
MAKE MY HEART SO HAPPY.

TO MY WONDERFUL HUSBAND...WHO'S LAST BUT NEVER, EVER, LEAST... I HAVE
LOVED YOU MY WHOLE LIFE AND WILL LOVE YOU FOR THE REST. YOU ARE MY
SOFT PLACE TO FALL, AND I AM SO GRATEFUL FOR OUR LOVE AFFAIR. THANK
YOU FOR ALWAYS SUPPORTING MY
CRAZY IDEAS AND GIVING ME EVERYTHING I COULD'VE EVER WANTED.
FOOD HAS ALWAYS BEEN AND ALWAYS WILL BE LOVE FOR US.

AFTERWORD

TO MY MOST WONDERFUL FAMILY AND FRIENDS,

AS I COME TO THE END OF THIS COOKBOOK, I FIND MYSELF REFLECTING ON THE CHERISHED MEMORIES AND FLAVORS THAT HAVE SHAPED MY FAMILY GATHERINGS THROUGHOUT THE YEARS. EACH RECIPE IN THIS COLLECTION CARRIES WITH IT A STORY~ A STORY OF LOVE, LAUGHTER, AND THE JOY OF SHARING MEALS TOGETHER.

OUR FAMILY TRADITIONS HAVE BEEN PASSED DOWN THROUGH GENERATIONS, AND THIS COOKBOOK REPRESENTS A LABOR OF LOVE TO PRESERVE AND SHARE THOSE TRADITIONS WITH ALL OF YOU. FROM PASTA TO SWEETS, THESE RECIPES ARE MORE THAN JUST DIRECTIONS ~ THEY ARE A PART OF WHO I AM TO MY CORE.

I HOPE THAT AS YOU FLIP THROUGH THE PAGES, YOU ARE INSPIRED TO CREATE YOUR OWN MEMORIES AROUND YOUR DINNER TABLE. MAY THESE RECIPES BRING WARMTH TO YOUR HOMES AND FILL YOUR HEARTS AS THEY HAVE OURS. WHETHER YOU'RE COOKING FOR A SPECIAL OCCASION OR SIMPLY A WEEKNIGHT MEAL, MAY THESE DISHES NOURISH BOTH BODY AND SOUL.

AS WE CONTINUE TO PASS THESE RECIPES DOWN TO FUTURE GENERATIONS, LET US REMEMBER THAT FOOD IS MORE THAN SUSTENANCE~ IT IS A CATALYST FOR LOVE, CONNECTION, AND CELEBRATION. MAY THIS COOKBOOK BE A TESTAMENT TO THE BONDS THAT UNITE US AND THE DELICIOUS TRADITIONS THAT WE HOLD SO CLOSE TO OUR HEARTS.

WITH LOVE AND GRATITUDE

Shelly

INDEX OF RECIPES

O

P

R

S

Z

Made in the USA
Las Vegas, NV
01 October 2024

f731a949-ff81-47d9-a437-afe2a5e195eaR01